MY ALLAH SERIES

MY GOD IS ALLAH

KISA KIDS PUBLICATIONS

AL-KISA FOUNDATION
WWW.KISAKIDS.ORG

PARENTS' CORNER

إِلَـٰهُكُمْ إِلَـٰهٌ وَاحِدٌ

...Your God is one God...
(Sūrat Hā-Mīm, Verse 6)

Dear Parents/Guardians,

Islām is based on the principle of *tawḥīd*, the oneness of Allāh. The first of the five *Uṣūl ad-Dīn*, the roots of religion, is *tawḥīd*. Allāh has created all of us with a pure *fiṭrah*, or innate nature, which recognizes the principle of *tawḥīd*. This *fiṭrah* is especially very strong and pure in children. The child's *fiṭrah* knows that there is one God, so the notion of *tawḥīd* does not need to be taught, but rather emphasized and strengthened in children.

As you read this book with your children, emphasize how irrational it is for anyone to worship anything other than Allāh, since everyone is in need and only Allāh can fulfill their needs! Only Allāh is needless and, therefore, worthy of worship!

With Du'as,
Kisa Kids Publications

Some people worship the sun, but the sun can be hidden by a small cloud.
"How can something that can be hidden be my God?!" I want to shout out loud!

Who created the sun?

Some people worship the moon, but it goes away during the day! How can we worship a moon that repeatedly fades away?

Can the moon create anything?

4

Some people worship animals that need food and water to survive.
How can we worship something that needs something else to stay alive?

What are some other things animals need to survive?

There is only one God, whom we call Allah.
He sent Prophet Muhammad (S) to teach us "La ilaaha illallaah."
We don't worship anyone or anything except Him.
Allah doesn't need us, but we all need Him!

How are the people in the picture worshipping Allah?

We should only pray to Allah, as He is our Creator.
Doing *sajdah* to Allah is how we worship our Master.

What are some things we can pray for when we make dua?

Allah is our God — He is the only one.
We worship only Him, not the moon or the sun.
He created everything that we see.
He takes care of us and gives us all that we need!

What did Allah give the little bird in the window to help it survive?